Oh, Behave!

Manners at Home

Siân Smith

www.raintreepublishers.co.uk
Visit our website to find out more information about Raintree books.

To order:
☎ Phone 0845 6044371
🖷 Fax +44 (0) 1865 312263
🖳 Email myorders@raintreepublishers.co.uk

Customers from outside the UK please telephone +44 1865 312262

Raintree is an imprint of Capstone Global Library Limited, a company incorporated in England and Wales having its registered office at 7 Pilgrim Street, London, EC4V 6LB – Registered company number: 6695582

Edited by Dan Nunn, Rebecca Rissman, and John-Paul Wilkins
Designed by Marcus Bell
Picture research by Elizabeth Alexander
Production by Alison Parsons
Originated by Capstone Global Library Ltd
Printed and bound in China by Leo Paper Products Ltd

ISBN 978 1 406 23820 4
16 15 14 13 12
10 9 8 7 6 5 4 3 2 1

British Library Cataloguing in Publication Data
Smith, Siân.
Manners at home. -- (Oh, behave!)
395.1'22-dc22
A full catalogue record for this book is available from the British Library.

Acknowledgements
We would like to thank the following for permission to reproduce photographs: © Capstone Publishers pp. 7, 11 (Karon Dubke); Alamy pp. 20, 22 (© Fancy); Corbis pp. 6 (© Ocean), 8, 22 (© moodboard), 18 (© Tiara Hobbs), 19) © Datacraft Co., Ltd.), 21 (© Tim Pannell); Getty Images pp. 13 (JGI/Jamie Grill/Blend Images), 14, 22 (Bernd Opitz/Taxi); iStockphoto pp. 5 (© Catherine Yeulet), 10 (© Pierre Yu), 12, 23 (© Julia Savchenko), 16, 22 (© Leigh Schindler); Shutterstock pp. 4, 15 (© Monkey Business Images), 9, 23 (© windu), 17 (© AISPIX).

Front cover photograph of boy looking at chocolate cake reproduced with permission of Alamy (© Fancy). Rear cover photograph reproduced with permission of istockphoto (© Pierre Yu).

Every effort has been made to contact copyright holders of material reproduced in this book. Any omissions will be rectified in subsequent printings if notice is given to the publisher.

We would like to thank Nancy Harris and Dee Reid for their assistance in the preparation of this book.

Contents

Good manners

People with good manners know how to behave in different places.

If you have good manners, people
will enjoy having you at home.

Coming home

Don't walk inside with mud on your shoes.

If you wipe your feet you will keep your home clean.

Looking after things

Don't climb on the furniture.

Sitting nicely will keep you and the things in your home safe.

Don't lie if you break something
by mistake.

It is better to tell the truth and say you are sorry.

Don't take things that belong to
other people.

Ask if you want to borrow something.
Remember to say "please" and
"thank you".

People at home

Don't keep things all to yourself.

When you share you make everyone happy.

Don't shout or be rude to people.

Talk politely to people and they will listen.

Don't wait for other people to tidy up after you.

Put your toys away when you have
finished playing with them.

Think about how you can help people at home.

People with good manners make a
home a nicer place to be.

Best behaviour

Which person here has good manners?

Answer on page 24

Picture glossary

borrow to use something that belongs to someone else

good manners ways of behaving politely and well

Index

Answer to question on page 22
The boy helping his dad with the washing up has good manners.

Notes for parents and teachers
Before reading
Explain that good manners are ways of behaving – they help us to understand what to do and how to act. They are important because they show us how to treat each other and help us to get on well with other people. What examples of good manners can the children think of? List these together.

After reading
- Help the children to be more conscious of the manners they use at home by asking them to take a photo or draw a picture of themselves demonstrating good manners at home. The photos and pictures can be made into a display. The children can explain what their picture shows and how behaving in that way made them and the people around them feel. Key words could be displayed around the photos.
- Give the children scenarios on manners at home and ask them what the best thing to do is. For example a boy whose younger sister is playing with one of his toys. What should he do? What if the toy is breakable? For example they could snatch the toy back, speak to their sister politely and give her a replacement toy, let a parent know, and so on.